Introducing – Harry
Rodger Webb, aged 2,
in India, 1943

CLIFFHISTORY

Written and Edited by Robin Morgan and Amy Turner
Design Director Stephen Reid
Picture Editor and research Patrick Llewellyn

First published in the United Kingdom in 2010 by:
Evans Mitchell Books
54 Baker Street,
London,
W1U 7BU
United Kingdom
www.embooks.co.uk
Copyright © 2010 Evans Mitchell Books

British Library Cataloguing in Publication Data
A CIP record of this book is available on request from
the British Library

ISBN: 978-1-901268-51-5

Printed in Germany

Evans Mitchell Books

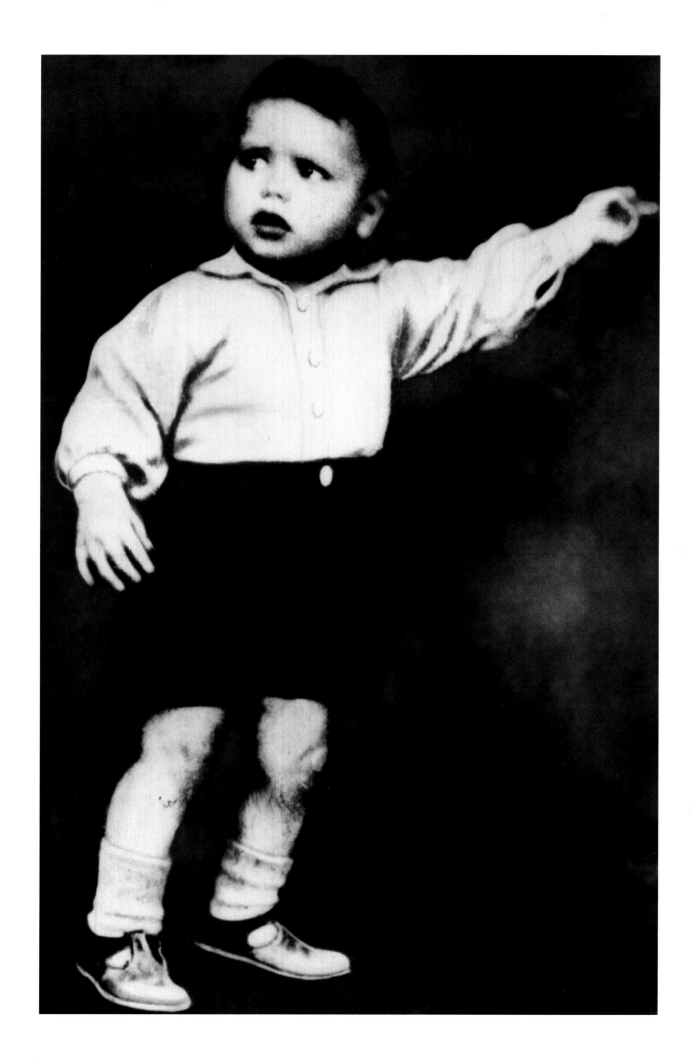

It began, as so many legends have since...
with a guitar. The year is 1957.
Dwight D. Eisenhower is inaugurated as
President of the United States for a second
term, Elvis Presley is energising the youth
of nations and as the Soviet Union launches
the Sputnik satellite, Rodger Webb comes
home to his wife Dorothy and their young
family with a gift for his 17-year-old son Harry.

The Cavern Club is about to open in Liverpool and two young schoolboys named Lennon and McCartney meet at a fete where they share an adolescent dream to form a band.

But long before the Merseybeat is born, the boy and his new guitar in the tiny bedroom of a semi-detached house in Cheshunt, Hertfordshire, begin a journey.

Cliff's parents, Rodger and Dorothy moved back to England after Indian independence in 1948

The journey will span decades and continents and inspire hearts and minds. It will accumulate hundreds of gold and platinum discs, 88 international entertainment awards, more than 250 million record sales, 10 box office hits and millions of minutes of airtime.

The accolades exhaust the imagination, but one will stand out, a testament to the relationship between one man and his audience. Surpassing The Beatles, Elvis Presley and every act that ever stood before a microphone and a packed house, this man will record No 1 hits in all the five decades since rock 'n' roll began. Who would bet against a sixth?

This is a record of that journey, the story of that boy, his shiny new guitar and a journey that continues on stage to this day. It has been chronicled countless times. But this is Cliff. His Story. In pictures.

Cliff at his parents' house in Cheshunt, Herts,1958. His career was just beginning to bloom

"I went on tour with a band of guys that were with me at school and it was obvious, professionally, that we weren't cutting it. So I recruited a guy called Hank Marvin and a guy called Bruce Welch and they became my guitarists.

"During that tour we met up with Jet Harris, who became my bass player. Then the three of them remembered a young drummer they jammed with in a club in London called Tony Meehan, and he joined us.

"Then, of course, I called our band The Drifters. We were not aware at that stage in 1958 of the American band, so quite rightly we bowed to them and gave up the name. And we chose the name The Shadows."

It took only weeks for Cliff Richard to make the leap from gigs in pubs and clubs to the hit parade and national television. British youth was screaming for its own homegrown cult figures. Record labels were scouring the dance halls to feed the national appetite of British youth and found Cliff touring venues such as the Regal Ballroom in Ripley, Derbyshire. He had the voice, the looks, the talent and the personality.

In 1958, a year after leaving school, Cliff was already gigging in dance halls

On 9 August he had been signed by Columbia Records, and before the month was out his first single, Move It, hit the charts. Originally it had been slated for the flipside to Schoolboy Crush, but legend has it that the daughter of Cliff's producer Norrie Paramor persuaded her father otherwise. The song shot to No 2 in the British charts. And, as Cliff embarked on his first UK Tour, critics were already hailing it as the first genuine British rock 'n' roll classic.

In 1959, Britain had awoken to a homegrown sensation. Move It was followed quickly with Living Doll and Travelling Light. The New Musical Express honoured Cliff as the Best New Singer.

The British press realized rock 'n' roll sold newspapers, and Cliff was front page news. The Daily Mirror reported on the phenomenon – his fans loved his eyes; dark, luminous and slumberous, while Reveille was impressed by his modesty. 'He Doesn't Try To be Sexy' was their headline. He didn't have to try. Cliff was raising the quizzical eyebrows of every parent in Britain who couldn't understand why their teenage daughters were screaming hysterically en masse at his every appearance.

And in the dance halls of Britain, young boys watched, learned and dreamed of emulating their idol. One was a young Paul McCartney who remembers being an avid fan. Men who were to become the biggest names in the rock 'n' roll hall of fame queued to watch him.

By 1959, Cliff and The Shadows had recorded three hit singles

"Before Move It there was nothing," John Lennon would say before his death. "A tremendous influence on my early days," said Freddie Mercury. Legends in their own right remember seeing Cliff on stage and have acknowledged his contribution to their careers.

From Bob Geldof to Sting, from Eric Clapton to Elton John, from Pete Townshend to Bert Weedon, the most exceptional talents that have ever performed remember the days, as the 50s closed and the 60s heralded a global cultural shift, when one name was on everyone's lips.

"It's never been said," says Bob Geldof, "but without Cliff and The Shads there's no English pop business." As George Harrison said, 'No Cliff and The Shadows, no Beatles.'

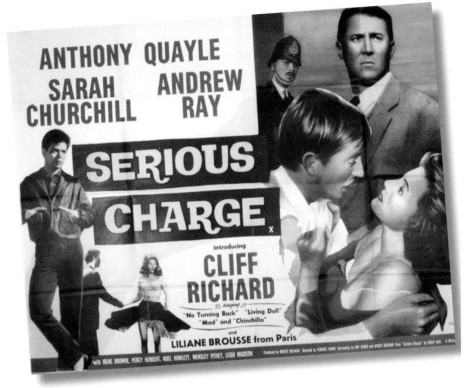

Cliff as Curley Thompson
in Serious Charge, 1959.
The film made Livin' Doll,
released the same year,
a hit for Cliff Richard and
The Shadows

Even as the ink dried on his recording contract, Cliff Richard's status as rock 'n' roll icon was generating excitement elsewhere. On tour he could only be in one place at a time, but in the cinema he could be on a thousand screens a night, playing to hundreds of thousands.

He was immediately cast in an edgy 1959 drama, Serious Charge, with Anthony Quayle. As Curley Thompson he played the younger brother of a thug, singing with The Drifters in coffee bar scenes.

Cliff only had to travel a few miles to the film set at the MGM Studios in Borehamwood and on location further up the A1, at Stevenage in Hertfordshire.

But Serious Charge included three numbers, and one, Living Doll, hit the No 1 spot for six full weeks, selling more than a million copies in the UK. It was also Cliff's first US hit.

1960 portrait by Harry Hammond, the first great photographer of British rock 'n' roll

That was quickly followed in 1960 with Expresso Bongo, adapted from a West End stage play and starring Cliff as a talented young musician who is discovered and exploited by a seedy promoter, played by Laurence Harvey. It was billed as a 'Brit Beat Classic' and was released across the USA, where the New York Times recoiled from its realism - and excited the interest of film censors.

Both were gritty, cynical dramas and reflected the changing social commentary and landscape of Britain – the war years had seen the birth of a new generation that was ready to question the status quo and liberate the aspirations of youth. The 60s revolution was in full swing and Cliff led the vanguard into a new age of cultural and social emancipation.

Onstage with The Shadows.
An early performance in their
rock 'n' roll phase, 1959

Sylvia Syms as stripper
Maisie King, Laurence
Harvey as talent scout
Johnny Jackson and Cliff
as young star Bongo
Herbert in the 1960 motion
picture Expresso Bongo

LAURENCE HARVEY
SYLVIA SYMS
YOLANDE DONLAN

Expresso Bongo A

CLIFF RICHARD

Written for the Screen by WOLF MANKOWITZ
Director and Produced by VAL GUEST
Distributed by BRITISH LION FILMS

LAURENCE HARVEY
SYLVIA SYMS
YOLANDE DONLAN

Expresso Bongo A

CLIFF RICHARD

Written for the Screen by WOLF MANKOWITZ
Director and Produced by VAL GUEST

The relationship turns sour
between Bongo Herbert
and his agent, Johnny
Jackson. Cliff and
Laurence Harvey filmed
at the Dorchester hotel in
Mayfair, London

May 1960: Cliff and
the singer Adam Faith
rehearse for the
Royal Command
Performance at Victoria
Palace Theatre, London

Fans mob Cliff as
he leaves a performance
in 1961. Looking
exhausted, Cliff heads
home in the back of a van

Within two years of Move It, Cliff was having to move it himself. Nine EPs, three albums, 14 singles – all of them huge hits – two movies and countless television appearances had created a worldwide fan base.

Along with Elvis, he was the biggest rock 'n' roll act in the business and took the show on the road, from Australia to America, in 1961. When he landed at Idlewild, later John F Kennedy airport, in New York, he was greeted by hysterical fans waving welcome placards.

It was only a few days short of his 21st birthday when Dorothy Webb helped her son pack for a six-week tour of Australia.

October 1961. A few days before his 21st birthday, Cliff's mother helps him pack for a six-week tour of Australia with The Shadows

But the hunger for Cliff's music was not restricted to touring. Merchandising arrived on the music scene, from posters to magazines and Cliff's face was everywhere – even on hearth rugs.

In between jetting around the world he recorded two more albums in the Abbey Road studios – Listen To Cliff and 21 Today – and four hit singles including his first Christmas No 1, I Love You.

The milestones of a career were planted in his wake, and Cliff was speeding along a highway littered with awards, hits and critical acclaim. Cliff was showing an unrivalled range of music, from a rocker's frantic pace to softer, relaxed ballads – raising the bar for other acts to follow in sustaining an audience's rapt attention.

He had his own TV show, top billing at the London Palladium and The Variety Club of Great Britain had voted him the nation's number one.

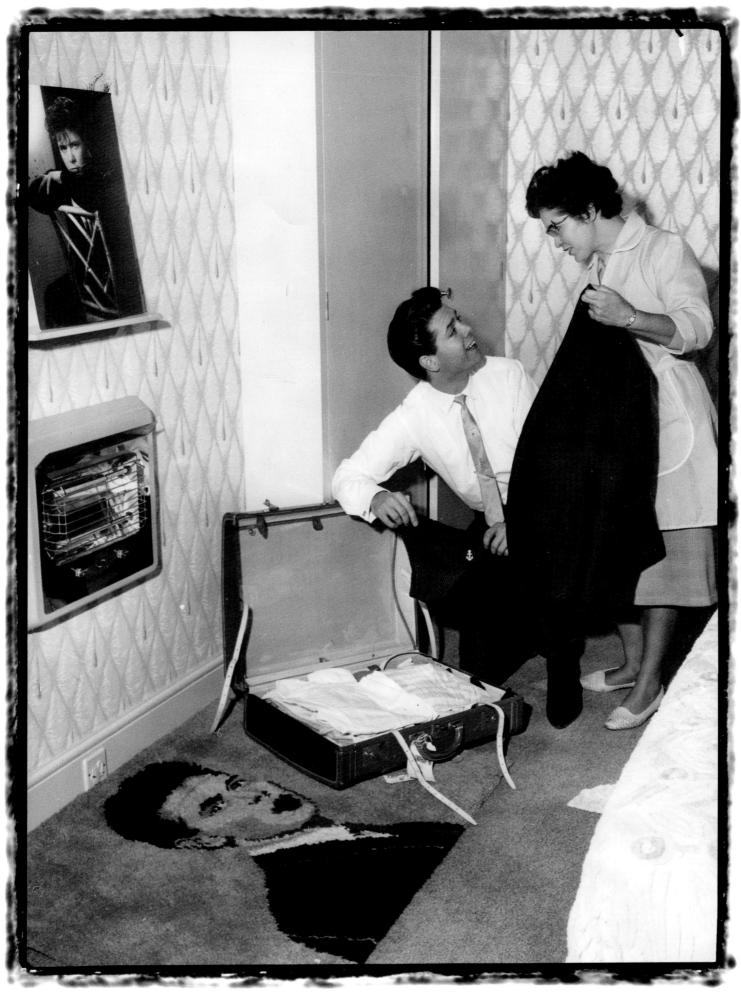

1961: Excited fans greet Cliff at Idlewild airport (now JFK) in New York, as he arrives for a six-week US tour

A ten minute walk from St John's Wood tube station in London, sat a Georgian townhouse built in 1891. Converted into studios by The Gramophone Company in 1931, Sir Edward Elgar conducted the London Symphony Orchestra in recordings there, as did Sir Malcolm Sargent. And then along came Cliff.

Signed to Columbia Records which had acquired the Abbey Road Studios he was the first rock 'n' roll act to establish the studio's legendary status in rock and pop history. One minute Mozart was being recorded, the next it was Move It.

He would go on to write his name in the studio's visitors' book 48 times, recording albums and singles there for more than 20 years.

Cliff listens to the playback of Theme for a Dream at Abbey Road. The song helped to cement his status as a mainstream pop star

For five years between 1963 and 1968 the studios were monopolized, as the charts were, by two acts; Cliff and The Shadows and The Beatles. As one band departed another would hold the door open. There was barely recording time for any other acts. Studio 2 became the epicentre of rock music and Cliff's name was etched on its walls.

It was Cliff, with his heavy schedule, who pioneered overnight recording sessions. In those days the sound engineers wore white coats, janitors brown overalls and apprentices signed indentures to learn their trade. In spite of the heavily unionized structure – only union members were allowed to set up microphones and touch the equipment – Cliff was able to record hit singles in sessions that were strictly adhered to; 10am to 1pm, 2.30pm to 5.30pm and 7pm to 10pm. Winston Churchill had visited and thought Abbey Road "a hospital".

May 1961: Cliff and
Shadows Hank Marvin
(front right) and
Bruce Welch (standing
with guitar), at Abbey
Road Studios .
Following pages:
Cliff records Theme
for a Dream in 1961. In the
early days he sometimes
recorded without The
Shadows to allow for
different music styles

After two critically acclaimed gritty dramas, 1961 saw Cliff flex his musical comedy muscles with the cinema release of The Young Ones. It was his first starring role; as Nicky Black with Carole Gray as the love interest.

Film buffs have speculated that the movie – released in the US as Wonderful to Be Young – was the inspiration behind the later cult movie The Blues Brothers, and its legacy included the hit BBC comedy of the same name.

It was a life-affirming, upbeat vehicle for Cliff's song and dance routines and it proved he could act, too. If previous movies had looked to cash in on his voice and appeal, The Young Ones tasked Cliff to carry the entire 108 minutes.

Cliff and Carole Gray rehearse with broomsticks for The Young Ones, 1961

It is a time capsule of early 60s rock 'n' roll and has been described by Hollywood insiders as the best British musical of all time. It was produced on a budget of £230,000 – a princely sum in 1961.

Loosely based on updating the plot of 'Babes In Arms' (the Rodgers and Hammerstein hit starring Mickey Rooney and Judy Garland), a young American singer on Broadway was initially tipped to star opposite Cliff, but the producers opted for homegrown talent – and Barbra Streisand stayed in New York.

It was an instant box office hit and helped sell more than a million copies of the chart-topping title song when it was released in January 1962. For the next two years, Cliff eclipsed Hollywood blockbusters as the official box office attraction in British cinema.

Cliff, Carole Gray and
Teddy Green in
The Young Ones, 1961

When Cliff and The Shadows toured Britain in 1962, the 23 venues sold out effortlessly. He was by far the biggest rock 'n' roll star of the day and, though he had softened his movie roles, critics to this day regard the tour as a landmark in rock 'n' roll history.

The tour was also notable for the decision, two-thirds of the way through its schedule, to release a live album. So memorable had been the earlier shows that Cliff's producers felt a live album must be recorded, if only for posterity's sake.

The venue was the ABC Kingston in southwest London where Cliff's performance was described as "blasting and blistering". It was a pioneering live album, raw and fresh in an age when acts were loath to record outside the comfort of a studio where rehearsal and repeats could smooth out rough edges.

Hank Marvin, Cliff, Bruce Welch and Tony Meehan onstage in 1962

To this day, Live At The ABC is regarded as the finest live album of the 60s and an original is a valuable collectors item.

That year Cliff charted a remarkable seven hit singles, recorded five EPs and the album 32 Minutes And 17 Seconds, selling millions of copies to a fan base that couldn't get enough.

Cliff was still only 21 but he was already preparing for another journey spanning 3,000 miles across five countries and a continent. The age of cheap transport for the masses and package holidays had arrived. British youth was discovering the world didn't end at Dover or Blackpool. That summer of 1962, a young band called The Rolling Stones made their debut at The Marquee Club in London, a drummer called Ringo Starr joined an up and coming band called The Beatles, the first live transatlantic television programme was broadcast, Nelson Mandela was arrested and Cliff learned to drive a bus.

Cliff with Helen Shapiro (left) and Rita Tushingham at the 1962 Showbiz awards. Helen and Rita shared the award for most promising newcomer. Cliff won Showbusiness Personality of the Year

There was no summer holiday for the biggest name in showbusiness in 1963. The movie of the same name had broken box office records in February, the title track would become a classic along with Bachelor Boy and Dancing Shoes, but Cliff still washed his own socks.

In March, Summer Holiday kept The Beatles' Please Please Me off the No 1 spot. The biggest live venue in British showbusiness in those days was the summer season at Blackpool. At the seaside town's newly opened ABC Theatre, Holiday Carnival starring Cliff and The Shadows played to packed houses of up to 4,000 a night for 16 weeks.

The Beatles were among the audience and that summer, Cliff, The Shadows and The Beatles got together at a party thrown by Bruce Welch and jammed together. Cliff himself performed The Beatles hit which he'd kept off the top spot in the charts that March.

Cliff hangs his socks to dry in the kitchen during a summer season at Blackpool, 1963

The newsreels of the day featured Cliff greeting fans who, inspired by Summer Holiday, had hired their own double decker bus they'd dubbed The Flying Haggis and driven to Blackpool.

That year an estimated 250,000 saw Cliff perform live in venues as far afield as Kenya, Spain and the USA where he appeared on the Ed Sullivan Show and performed to millions of viewers.

But it was the movie and the music that dominated the year. Summer Holiday remains one of the most refreshing, memorable and infectious films ever produced by British cinema – even if the crowds at the premier prevented its star from reaching the screening.

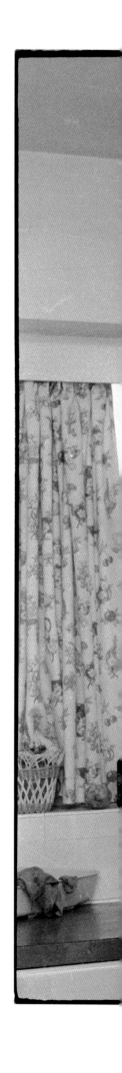

Cliff's most famous role: as Don in the musical Summer Holiday, 1963. This scene was filmed at Aldenham bus depot, Hertfordshire

ELSTREE DISTRIBUTORS LIMITED present
CLIFF RICHARD · LAURI PETERS
in "SUMMER HOLIDAY" (U)
with DAVID KOSSOFF
Guest Star RON MOODY and THE SHADOWS
A CINEMASCOPE PICTURE IN TECHNICOLOR
Produced by Kenneth Harper
Released through Warner-Pathe Distributors Ltd

ELSTREE DISTRIBUTORS LIMITED present
CLIFF RICHARD · LAURI PETERS
in "SUMMER HOLIDAY" (U)
with DAVID KOSSOFF
Guest Star RON MOODY and THE SHADOWS
A CINEMASCOPE PICTURE IN TECHNICOLOR
Produced by Kenneth Harper
Released through Warner-Pathe Distributors Ltd

On the set of Summer
Holiday in Athens,
Greece. The film's title
song reached number
one in the UK

Cliff and The Shadows enjoy a picnic with their entourage in Blackpool

Heartthrob on holiday:
Cliff draws in the sand on
Blackpool beach

On tour in 1963 – Cliff working tirelessly on a career that now spanned stage and screen

Britain's biggest hearthrobs in 1963 were Cliff and The Saint, later 007, Roger Moore

Cliff at the BBC
TV studios in
London, April 1963

No sooner had Cliff returned the No 9 bus – 'Piccadilly to South of France' – to the Aldenham bus depot, than he was embarking on another frenzied schedule from the television studios of Britain and America to film sets in Gran Canaria and North West Africa.

The tagline for Wonderful Life was "Cliff's back! He's swinging, singin', livin' and dancin' to a dozen tunes." It was the third hit in a row for Cliff's fresh new musical movie genre and was released in the USA as 'Swingers' Paradise'.

Almost half a century later in the digital age, an internet search reveals half a million sites listing the movie and its songs, with its stand-out song and dance number, On The Beach, commanding 390,000 references alone.

Cliff poses at the
wheel of his Corvette,
August 1963

Cliff is mobbed by fans as he arrives at the premiere of Summer Holiday at the Warner Theatre, Leicester Square in 1963. Concerned about security, police sent Cliff away. He watched the film at his manager's house in Maida Vale

Cliff's image-makers were working harder than ever to keep up with the public's insatiable demand. News photographers, reporters, magazines and television shows clamoured for the latest news about "Cliff".

From the delivery of a shiny new Corvette to a game of snooker at home with friends and family, every image was guaranteed to sell newspapers and the phrase 'photo-opportunity' came into its own.

It's All In The Game – Cliff enjoyed five Top 10 hits in 1964

Cliff couldn't appear in public without hordes of fans and photographers swarming to pay homage. Others might have wilted under the pressure and the constant demands, but Cliff's stamina and work ethic seemed inexhaustible.

1964 saw five top ten hits in the UK charts compared to The Beatles' three, and for the third successive year the New Musical Express readers voted him Top Male Singer, while the US Billboard Magazine awarded him Best Recording Artist.

Cliff starring as Johnnie
in the 1964 musical
Wonderful Life, about a
group of young popsters
filming in the desert

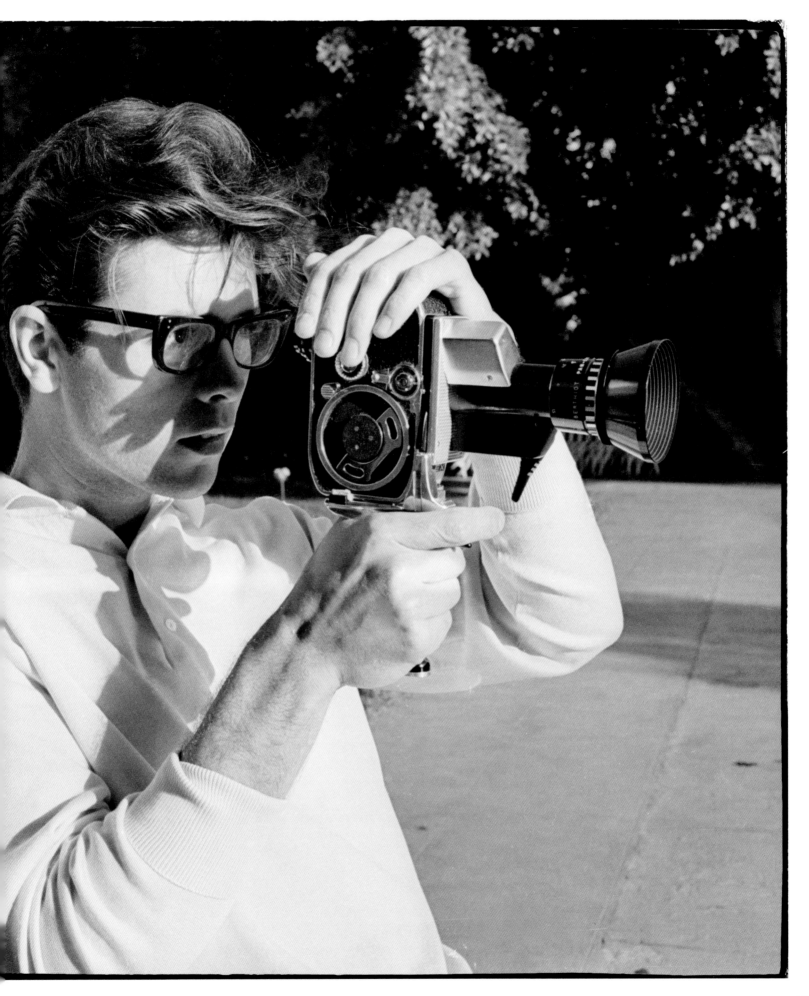

Hollywood's search for a new blonde bombshell produced Jayne Mansfield, and a fleeting novelty of the 60s was her aspirations as a singer. Columbia/EMI released a compilation album titled 5 Star Party with Cliff and The Shadows, Russ Conway and The Dave Clark Five, with Mansfield herself in a classic pin-up pose on the cover.

Curiously, Mansfield's musical career, though less than short lived, did include two songs: Suey and As The Clouds Drift By, which featured a young bass and lead guitarist called Jimi Hendrix.

But as her star was rapidly waning (the mini-skirt, Jean Shrimpton and Twiggy were consigning platinum blondes and cleavage to the cultural wilderness), Cliff's popularity was not only weathering the storm of Beatlemania and the new contenders for his throne, but consistently outperforming them.

With actress Jayne Mansfield, who appeared on the cover of a Columbia Records compilation which featured Cliff and The Shadows

The Shadows had reached their own pinnacle of fame and Cliff was increasingly performing alone and experimenting with his music. But he was also undergoing a life-changing metamorphosis that would define his life, his work and his ideals.

In 1965 Cliff declared his Christian faith and thought deeply about quitting his rock 'n' roll career. He was rumoured to have considered becoming a teacher. No-one could have blamed him for taking time out. For seven years he had given himself to music and his fans on an exhausting roller coaster ride from obscurity to fame. He was still only 24.

But it wasn't the end, it was merely a new beginning. A bigger journey beckoned with new peaks to climb, new records to achieve and fresh avenues to explore. Cliff had crested the wave of the early 60s across the entertainment industry. What was left to achieve?

Cliff in Wonderful Life,
Gran Canaria, 1964.
The trio of films made him
the UK's biggest box office
draw of the decade

By the mid 60s, Cliff Richard – the boy considered 'too sexy for television' – had grown into a man with his own ideas about how he wished to live and work. At 24, he was a learned veteran of the entertainment industry with the power to make decisions for himself.

Cliff made choices now that weren't just about chart and box office success. It was a time of artistic freedom and exploration. He starred in a one-hour television special with Liza Minelli, and conquered that other bastion of British entertainment – one that is widely regarded as the stage's toughest discipline – the pantomime.

June 1964: 18-year-old Liza Minelli, in London to make her debut on British TV, chats to Cliff during a break in filming

Aladdin at the London Palladium was just one of the new ventures he explored. His Christian faith did nothing to dilute his appeal. In 1965, with Elvis on the wane and The Beatles on everyone's lips, Cliff toured Europe, recorded two more television specials, topped the charts with The Minute You're Gone and was again voted Top Male Singer by readers of the music papers.

Two albums, three EPs and six singles were released that year and the work continued unabated. Film scripts were still piling up in the post but Cliff was no longer merely Britain's biggest popstar. He was maturing into a figure of national importance and influence beyond his status in film and music.

His views and his faith merely served to widen his appeal beyond his fan base. He was fast becoming a national institution.

Few photographs illustrate the charm and intimacy of the 60s as much as this rare shot of Cliff. Shaving in the mirror of his hotel room on tour with The Shadows, it speaks to an era when stardom had no need for muscled minders.

In the 60s, the relationship between a star of Cliff's magnitude and the press was one of mutual trust and respect. For the media he was news and for Cliff, the newspapers were a vital component in nurturing his relationship with his fans.

The legendary photographer Terry O'Neill, who chronicled the swinging 60s, describes it as an age of innocence. He first photographed bands like The Beatles and The Rolling Stones before they had hits. He was the first Fleet Street photographer assigned to seeking out the fresh new acts.

Life on the road: Cliff shaves in his hotel room, 1964

"Cliff started all that," he says. "He sold newspapers, and the editors were screaming for images of him. We were young and the world was our oyster. I could be a photographer, Cliff a musician, Michael Caine an actor. We were having the time of our lives, but we all thought the 60s –the music, the fashion – would end, and then we'd have to get a proper job."

In that climate, the stars and photographers were friends and acquaintances, young people surfing a cultural wave, travelling together, hanging out together, back stage and on the road; no cordons, no VIP areas and no paparazzi. Phrases like 'invasion of privacy' and 'off the record' were irrelevant.

Cliff with the Shadows
Hank Marvin and Brian
Bennett before a
performance, 1965

The trappings of success:
Cliff shows off his
left-hand-drive Corvette
Stingray, 1965

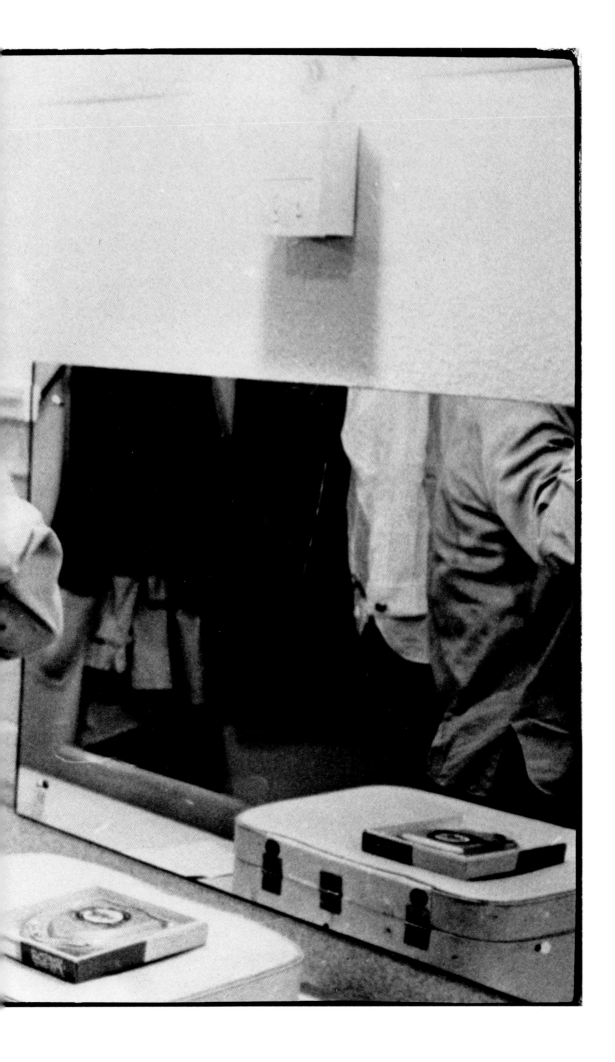

Backstage, February 1966: Cliff dresses for a performance

Stage hands:
Cliff and The Shadows'
set up before a
concert in 1966

In 1966 a new Cliff emerged. The Elvis flick was about to be shorn and Finders Keepers, the last of Cliff's upbeat musicals featuring The Shadows, was released. A year of transition was complete.

As the picture on the right shows, a more reflective and determined Cliff was redefining his stardom. On 16 June, he appeared on stage with the evangelist Billy Graham and spoke of his Christian faith.

At the time, the newspapers speculated that this heralded an end to his career. Fans wept openly and, it transpired, unnecessarily. Faith and fun, humility and humour, religion and rock 'n' roll were not mutually exclusive. And Cliff was the first major public figure to prove it.

In 1966 Cliff spoke for the first time about his faith

By now Cliff and The Shadows were having their strings pulled by puppet masters making the movie Thunderbirds Are Go (see next page). He was planning a tour of Japan and preparing for his first starring role as a straight actor.

In Two A Penny, Cliff played a thief who stole drugs from his mother's employer and was romantically involved with a similarly amoral girlfriend. Both are redeemed. The movie set the tone for an outspoken and motivated Cliff, who condemned the increasingly fashionable use of drugs by pop stars and increasing pre-marital promiscuity fuelled by the wide availability of the contraceptive pill.

Four more EPs and three more Top 10 hits kept him on top of the readers' polls for top British singer for the sixth year running.

1966: Cliff meets the
puppets Cliff Richard Jnr
and The Shadows,
from the film
Thunderbirds Are Go

And the winner is... In 1967 Cliff Richard was voted Britain's Best Dressed Man, an accolade that was repeated three years on the trot. He had captured the hearts of teenagers; both they and he, had matured over 10 years.

Glamorous and groomed, he had emerged as an accomplished all round entertainer and the parents of his fans were taking to the clean cut young man as an antidote to an age when psychedelic drugs and permissiveness were beginning to erode values and morality.

The same year, colour television was introduced to Britain, with the new cameras recording the Wimbledon finals on BBC2. Initially, four hours of colour television a week was scheduled, but within a year every BBC2 programme was broadcast in colour. BBC1 followed six months later.

The advent of colour TV revolutionized entertainment – the era of the television blockbuster was upon us. Colour sets disappeared from shop shelves as fast they could be manufactured. Sales soared from 275,00 in the first year to 12 million by the early 70s.

It was the new Mecca for entertainment; dancehalls closed as did cinema screens and Cliff was set to become the first major star of British television, commanding audiences in their millions.

Cliff and The Shadows
starred as themselves
in the rock and
roll comedy Finders
Keepers, 1966

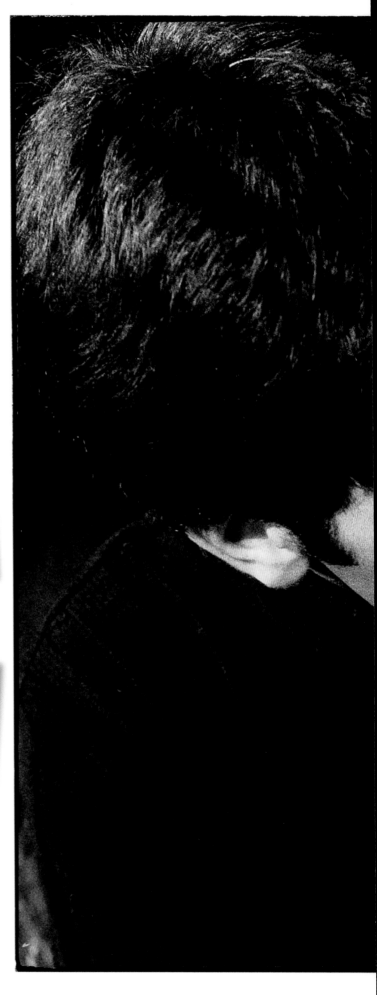

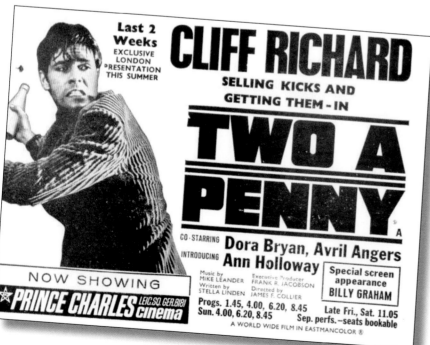

Cliff with Sandie Shaw.
He sang for Britain in the
1968 Eurovision Song
Contest, and she in 1967

In 1968 The Eurovision Song Contest ranked as the biggest non-sporting television event of the year, with audience figures (that have fluctuated since) in their hundreds of millions. That year also saw one of the greatest frauds in entertainment history.

Sandie Shaw had won for Britain in 1967 with Puppet On A String, which polled a record number of votes and Britain's first victory in the contest. The role of UK representative passed to Cliff in 1968.

Congratulations was the favourite from the moment Cliff gave voice to the song. Newspapers across Europe speculated only on what song would come second.

Cliff led the voting throughout the night with 400million people watching, and with all but Germany's vote cast,

Congratulations was in order. But suddenly and inexplicably, Germany awarded the Spanish entry – a kitsch number uniquely named La La La – the six points it needed to steal the glory by just one point.

It would be 40 years before the scandal – one of television's greatest – was fully exposed, but the result did nothing to dim the success of the song. Congratulations topped charts across Europe and earned Cliff his fifth gold disc.

In West Germany, which had voted for the Spanish entry, Congratulations led the charts for seven weeks.
Forty years later Cliff and Congratulations would be chosen as the title song in a show to celebrate the Eurovision's half century – and the scandal came to light.

March 1968: Cliff and Cilla Black count viewers' votes for the Song For Europe contest

Cliff readies himself backstage at the Eurovision Song contest in 1968

'How Franco Cheated Cliff Out Of The Eurovision Title' was the headline Britain woke up to in May 2008, 40 years after the event. The revelation solved a mystery – and suspicions that had festered over the decades.

A Spanish documentary-maker had revealed that executives of Spain's state-run television network had toured Europe in the run-up to the competition in 1968, on the orders of the dictator General Franco.

Their mission was to 'persuade' the other European television companies to vote for Spain's entry.

The winner of the competition was decided by a jury of 10, chosen by broadcasters from each of the 17 countries participating. Each member awarded one point to their favourite song.

Cliff performs Congratulations at the Eurovision Song Contest, April 1968 – broadcast in colour for the first time

With the emerging tourist industry on the Spanish Costas, Franco's regime hoped that a Eurovision win would boost its popularity both at home and abroad.

It seemed far from accidental that Congratulations should be pipped at the post by a single vote, and the documentary maker, Montse Fernandez Villa, was unequivocal when unveiling the results of her research.

"Televisión Española executives travelled around Europe buying series that would never be broadcast and signing concert contracts with odd, unknown groups and singers. These contracts were translated into votes. It was these bought votes that won Eurovision".

Cliff, on tour in Germany at the time, was philosophical. An official investigation 'would not be worth the trouble' he commented.

Congratulations was to lose by just 'un point' but music lovers cast their own vote and the song topped the charts across Europe

Cliff was vindicated by the overwhelming success of Congratulations, which became one of the biggest selling singles of all time, flying off the shop shelves and into Europe's charts.

And the suspicions aroused at the time resulted in a radical overhaul of the judging process.

But Eurovision and the advent of colour television pointed the way for the next chapter in Cliff history. Suddenly, viewing figures in their millions were achievable, bringing the Cliff adored by the public in film and on stage, into their homes.

As always, Cliff was in huge demand and extended his range, which included performing gospel concerts for the first time. Congratulations was joined by three more singles that year and three more albums, including another live album from his tour of Japan.

June 1968: Cliff and The Shadows accept their platinum discs from EMI, after Congratulations topped international charts

The public demand for television specials resulted in a 'Cliff At The Movies' special, for which he playfully posed in jungle tableaux. It was the beginning of Cliff's new career as the biggest star on British television, further widening his audience.

Cliff was now collaborating with friends such as Cilla Black and other artists, which led to a decade of Bank Holiday specials; Saturday Night In with Cliff and friends, and his shows consistently topped television viewing charts.

Cliff dresses as Tarzan for a London Weekend Television special, 'Cliff at the Movies', September 1968

Cliff with his E-type
Jaguar, 1969

Cliff was the male singer who captured the hearts and minds of the burgeoning television audiences, but his close friend for more than 40 years, Cilla Black, was a match for his popularity.

It was on Cilla's television show that Cliff first sang Congratulations, prior to its selection as Britain's Eurovision entry. The pair dominated British screens for years, sharing an incomparable bond in showbusiness, and a friendship that continues to this day.

The two share each other's company regularly. Both have holiday homes on Barbados, Cilla is a regular guest at Cliff's home in Portugal and they attend social events such as Wimbledon together.

Cilla recently recalled that, as a young Liverpudlian breaking onto the music scene, every girl she knew wanted to marry Cliff. "We still do," she joked in a television interview.

In the history of British television, no-one has ever enjoyed the sustained success of Cilla and Cliff in their separate shows, which regularly compelled audiences comprising a third of the UK population to tune in on Saturday nights.

Cliff and Una Stubbs arrive for a private reception at 10 Downing Street, March 1970
Opposite: with actress Margo Jenkins, May 1971. Cliff was due to appear on stage in The Potting Shed at Bromley Theatre, Kent, but the venue burned down

Another of the enduring friendships that have characterized Cliff's life began in the early 70s, when Cliff invited a young singer, Olivia Newton John, onto his television show.

Olivia was romantically involved with Bruce Welch when she met Cliff, but when she broke up with The Shadows' guitarist, the bond she had formed with Cliff sparked widespread speculation that they would marry.

With 22-year-old Olivia Newton-John who had just released her first single, If Not For You. They were pictured at the Music Echo Awards where Cliff was voted a close second to Tom Jones in the Best Male category. February 1971

But her own career was exploding on the back of regular appearances on Cliff's television shows and Hollywood beckoned Olivia, who would go onto to star with John Travolta in Grease, one of the greatest box office musicals of all time.

"Cliff was the man who opened doors for me," she has always said. Cliff, who prides himself on his iron-clad discretion, loyalty to his friends and their privacy, admitted in a BBC interview in 2003 that he was in love with Olivia.

"At the time when I and many of us were in love with Olivia she was engaged to someone else," Cliff said. "I'm afraid I lost the chance."

Steadfast as ever, he did not expand upon the statement, leaving the press to speculate that he had felt uncomfortable extending the relationship out of respect for his friend Bruce Welch.

Within a few months of his father's death in 1961, Cliff believes a void opened up in his life that would remain for years to come. Neither fame nor money filled it. Eventually faith would.

He had begun reading the bible after meeting Jehovah's Witnesses on an American tour in 1962. Shortly after, his former English and Drama teacher introduced him to the Religious Instruction teacher at his old school.

The meeting was the catalyst for what were perhaps Cliff's two most enduring relationships outside of his family – the first with Christianity, the second with that teacher; Bill Latham.

On 7 March 1971, 1500 people turned up to hear Cliff's hour-long sermon and song session at Queen's Road Baptist Church, Coventry

But it would be five years or more before Cliff realised he had found the faith he needed to fill the void left by the death of the father he adored.

As he began to record Gospel music and prepared to announce his conversion, Cliff was conscious that there was a risk of commercial suicide – rock music and God seemed strange bedfellows to the media of the day, trapped as they were, and still are, in their own stereotypes.

But there was another revelation: his fans and the public didn't give a fig for the caricatures that the media invariably draw of the famous. The music kept coming and the fans kept filling the seats.

The two most notable changes in Cliff? He felt happier and, as a friend noted, he "stopped using the F-word".

In 1972, the world saw a stream of firsts. The first pocket calculator went on sale for $400, something called a 'video game' was released, women were finally recruited as FBI agents, and Cliff was banned from Singapore because he had 'long hair'.

Was the world going mad? Cliff's single Sing A Song Of Freedom was banned by South Africa's apartheid regime. The lyrics could hardly be described as an incitement to violent insurrection:

If you're looking for an answer, it's very close at hand
Just take a look around you and then you'll understand
Clap your hands together and let me hear the sound
It's the time for liberation, so pass the word around

But Cliff had made a stand during tours of South Africa, when the authorities had tried to stop him playing to multi-racial audiences, which did not endear him to bigots.

Perversely, Cliff's insistence on touring apartheid South Africa with his Christian message, and his determination to engage with the oppressed black majority through the unifying message of Christianity, also saw his name ludicrously posted on a UN 'blacklist' of celebrities who had visited South Africa and somehow "aided and abetted" the regime.

But that year also saw Cliff in a huge hit BBC series, 'It's Cliff Richard', during which, for one episode, Mary Hopkin came out of retirement. It was apparent to all that Cliff was enjoying his new career as television's biggest draw.

Cliff rehearses the
infamous sailor sketch
with Eric Morecambe
and Ernie Wise for
The Morecambe and
Wise show, 1973

"TAKE ME HIGH" starring CLIFF RICHARD with DEBBIE WATLING, HUGH GRIFFITH, GEORGE COLE
Music and Lyrics by Tony Cole   Screenplay by Christopher Penfold   Produced by Kenneth Harper   Directed by David Askey
Technicolor ®   released by MGM ⊕ EMI

"TAKE ME HIGH" starring CLIFF RICHARD with DEBBIE WATLING, HUGH GRIFFITH, GEORGE COLE
Music and Lyrics by Tony Cole   Screenplay by Christopher Penfold   Produced by Kenneth Harper   Directed by David Askey
Technicolor ®   released by MGM ⊕ EMI

Cliff stars in Take Me High
with Hugh Griffith and
Anthony Andrews, 1974

July 1979: Cliff celebrates
21 years in show business
with friends including
Anita Harris, Brian Bennett,
Bruce Welch, Christopher
Timothy, Joan Collins,
Hank Marvin, Kenny
Everett, Elaine Paige, Patti
Boulaye and Lionel Blair

At the end of the 70s and into the 80s, Cliff enjoyed a huge international renewal reaching new audiences with his music, particularly Devil Woman, Miss You Nights and the album I'm Nearly Famous. We Don't Talk Anymore was a Number One hit and his duet Suddenly with Olivia Newton John made the US Top 20. But outside of music, faith and family there were two new loves and they came as a package. Tennis and Sue Barker.

It was probably the closest Cliff ever got to marriage. He has since confessed there was a time when being wed was all he wanted, "... when I was really young and with The Shadows, and girls were throwing themselves at us. The Shads all got married and I thought 'Help! I'm the only one left'. They were all having babies and I just felt left out.

"Had marriage come my way, I would have had to change my life completely. I would have had to ask my partner 'Are you going to tour with me? And what about children. Would they have gone too?"

With tennis star Sue Barker at a tennis tournament in Beckenham, Kent, June 1983

Cliff and Sue both had hectic schedules with weeks and even months apart. Their relationship shifted a gear and while the romance waned, their friendship didn't. And one significant legacy – other than Cliff learning to play tennis – was the Cliff Richard Tennis Development Trust, which sent experts around schools to identify and financially support budding champions. The Trust also encouraged children with physical handicaps to take up the sport.

It was at one pro-celebrity tournament that Cliff remembers the only time he has been booed in his life: "I was serving to a girl in a wheelchair and accidentally aced her."

Tennis wasn't the only beneficiary of Cliff's generosity. Since his early career he has given more and more of his time and his money to causes close to his heart, and charity work has become one of the most consuming and defining passions of his life.

It started with fund-raising gospel concerts for disaster relief in 1968, along with an organisation called Tearfund. The Cliff Richard Charitable Trust, founded over 40 years ago, received the profits from one in every ten concerts Cliff performed. Increasingly, he would request donations to the charity in return for singing at events, and today the Trust supports more than 200 causes every year, both at home and abroad, from Bangladesh to Brazil.

With tennis player Annabel Croft

Priority is given to charities working in medical research, with children and the elderly, and those involved with the physically or mentally disabled.

One unique result of Cliff's popularity is the dozens of Cliff Richard Meeting Houses around the world, in which his fan base became not only organised Cliff-appreciation societies but fund raisers for the Trust.

As Cliff has said in his autobiography: "I'm always bowled over by my fans' ingenuity and generosity. My fans have followed me not just through my music but through my lifestyle."

The cake's the clue. It isn't Cliff's game. The spiky-haired marzipan character in Scotland's national soccer strip bears a striking resemblance to the host.

1986 started with Rod Stewart's birthday party in January – but it was to be a huge celebration for Cliff's career too.

Cliff was in rehearsal for Time, Dave Clark's sci-fi epic, at London's Dominion Theatre. The show had broken all records for advance bookings and Cliff's year-long run had completely sold out.

It was one of the country's biggest theatre venues with

Cliff and George Michael admire the birthday cake at Rod Stewart's party at Stringfellows nightclub, 1986

seating for over 2,000, and shows had always been hard -pushed to sustain a capacity audience over many months. Cliff's popularity changed that.

The stage had to be substantially remodelled to accommodate an extravagant set which relied heavily on special effects and hydraulics. It was a gruelling test of Cliff's stamina but the self confessed Star Trek fan, Cliff, played to more than 750,000 people during his run.

Cliff remembers often leaving the theatre after the show to play midnight tennis with fellow cast members. "I loved our camaraderie", he says. He recalls Time as a "frolic, one of the greatest years of my life". But he must have been running on adrenalin. It wasn't until his run ended that he realised how exhausted he was.

Cliff re-released
Living Doll with The Young
Ones for Comic Relief, 1986

What started out as a charity idea became another huge hit with the team behind one of the defining cult comedy classics of the 80s.

Cliff re-recorded Living Doll with the stars of the hit BBC comedy, named after one of his hits - The Young Ones.

The show, with Rik Mayall and Nigel Planer, began the writing career of Ben Elton and featured Mayall as a student fan of Cliff's. And Cliff's hit was the title song that introduced the show.

The re-recorded hit went to No 1, raising money for Comic Relief, but there were more collaborations that year. Cliff recorded with Elton John and Sarah Brightman. And a charity recording, Live In World, featured Cliff with Dave Stewart, Steve Harley, Elkie Brooks, Kim Wilde and a host of musicians and singers.

How Cliff found the time in 1986 to do anything else remains a mystery. And yet he continued to give his time to charities, appearing before 250,000 in London's Hyde Park, for Sport Aid.

Cliff as rock star Chris Wilder in the musical Time, with fellow cast members Jodie Wilson, Dawn Hope and Maria Ventura at the Dominion theatre, April 1986

Cliff and actor Bob
Hoskins lend their support
to publicise a charity drive
to the Sahara

Cliff gathers with composer Lionel Bart (left) and record producer Alan Tarney (right) to celebrate his Ivor Novello award for 30 years in showbusiness with Bill Martin, co-writer of Congratulations

Evil, obsessive, violent? Cliff as Heathcliff? Ten years after he handed over the lead in Time to David Cassidy, Cliff found himself facing the most challenging and unlikely title role on a West End stage.

It was brave and audacious, a man steeped in Christian values would take on the mantle of one devoid of them; a lustful, vicious, wuthering monster who knew no boundaries, who had no filters and who observed no faith. Could he pull it off? Would an audience be convinced?

Cliff was determined, so determined he sank millions of his own money into the venture. It toured first in Birmingham, then Edinburgh, Manchester and London, playing to more than half a million people.

Cliff meets David Cassidy who took over his role in the West End musical Time, in June 1987

People camped out in freezing temperatures for premier tickets, advance bookings totalled £8.5million and he played to packed houses. The show had already recouped its investment half way through the tour.

One of the fiercest critics and sharpest eyes in showbusiness, the lyricist Tim Rice, simply observed, "you're an actor".

Heathcliff gave Cliff the most rewarding achievement of his career, for the first time in his life, and in his career, he got to play a scowling, vile, and hateful man. "I loved every minute of it," he said.

Bruce Welch, Cliff and Hank Marvin onstage in 1989. That year they played to 144,000 fans over two nights at Wembley Stadium

The 90s was a decade when Cliff stretched himself in all directions; on stage, television, at Royal Variety performances, in video, at rock concerts and on tours to New Zealand, Australia, Europe, Britain and Ireland.

At the start of that decade, he filled the NEC Birmingham and Wembley Arena to capacity, all on consecutive nights. He played the Knebworth rock festival, and topped the charts with his Christmas single, Saviour's Day.

The CD format was being introduced and all 36 Cliff albums were re-released in 1992. The next year, Cliff Richard: The Album soared straight to No 1. Now 35 years into his career he was still topping the charts, touring to packed houses and breaking new ground.

Cliff making the video for Saviour's Day – his number one hit of 1990

The groundwork on Heathcliff had begun in 1994 but Cliff continued to tour the northern and southern hemispheres, and in 1995 he appeared as one of the principal artists at the VE Day anniversary celebrations in front of Buckingham Palace singing to an audience that crammed The Mall and filled Trafalgar Square.

That year he became Sir Cliff Richard, knighted for his services to charity, although it could so easily have been for his pioneering role in British rock 'n' roll, his services to entertainment or indeed the nation.

Clockwise from top: Cliff with Diana Ross at Heathrow airport. With actress and model Iman at the London premiere of Star Trek VI in 1992. With Joan Collins at the Waldorf hotel in 2001, for the opening night party for her new play, Over the Moon. With Marty Wilde at the Good Rocking Tonight Party, tribute to Jack Good, 1992. Right: With Elton John at the Nordoff Robbins music therapy concert at Knebworth, 1990

February 1994;
Ciff holds a press
conference to
announce plans to
play the lead in a rock
music version of
Wuthering Heights

Cliff, Elaine Paige and Des O'Connor meet the Queen at the 1995 Royal Variety Performance at the Dominion Theatre, London

Cliff plays Heathcliff in Wuthering Heights, October 1996. Helen Hobson plays Cathy

Right: Cliff poses for a Sunday Times Magazine cover story

Cliff Richard with
his sisters, left to right
Donna, Joan and
Jacqui, after receiving
his knighthood at
Buckingham
Palace in 1995

With the tennis match
rained off, Cliff stages an
impromptu concert at
Wimbledon in 1996

Cliff listens intently at a recording session with Austrian producer and keyboard player Peter Wolf, 1997.

The West End stage, impromptu concerts at rainswept Wimbledon, investitures at Buckingham Palace; it's easy to forget that, in his 50s, Cliff showed no signs of slowing down. Music is and always was paramount.

At an age when everyone takes stock, Cliff at 60 could look back on a career that was an endless narrative of success, achievement and growth: more than 60 albums, 65 top ten hits and 14 No 1s.

And he had ended the decade, his 60th year with another – the Millennium Prayer. It was arranged and recorded for charity. EMI, Cliff's label, had declined to release it, and radio stations also failed to see its potential, but – as always – the public had their own idea of what music they wanted to hear.

Cliff released it through an independent label and it stormed the charts – the song staying on top for three weeks to become his third highest selling single of all time. It sold over 1 million copies. It stayed in the charts at home and abroad for months and £1 million went to charity.

Yet again the public had voiced their appreciation and approval and showed no sign of letting up in their desire for more.

In 1998 Cliff had embarked on what would be one of the hardest working years of his career. It was his 40th year in showbusiness, with the Heathcliff album topping charts for eight weeks, and six million viewers tuning into his Christmas BBC special.

He toured for two months with Olivia Newton John, performed in the tribute concert for Princess Diana at Althorp, sold out a six week season at the Royal Albert Hall, recorded music videos and was acclaimed with Lifetime Achievement awards on the international stage.

He had the health and vitality of a man half his age. The pace was relentless yet the pressure seemed merely to be fuel to his drive. What kept him going?

Cliff with Elaine Paige and actress Wendy Richard at the London Variety Club luncheon in December 1998

Since he'd turned 50, Cliff recalls in his autobiography, his insurance company had insisted on frequent medicals – for no other reason than they couldn't afford to have him fall ill on tour. Cliff did, and still does pass them with flying colours. "If I have one burning ambition left it is to have a game of tennis on my hundredth birthday," he has said.

Scientific surveys have shown that people with faith tend to be happier, healthier and live longer. They can more easily cope with and mitigate stress, work more productively and relax more easily, ironing out the creases in life.

As he records in My Life, My Way, "I always feel I must be a disappointment to my doctor".

Tragedy and death were no strangers to Cliff. He had lost his father to a heart attack, as well as dear friends, and his charity work abroad in the Third World had exposed him to suffering and mortality.

But nothing prepared him for the brutal murder of his close friend Jill Dando in April 1999. His faith has given him no fear of death himself, but Cliff admits he finds the loss of others harder to bear, and the loss of Dando was devastating.

They had met when Cliff accepted an invitation to accompany her at the Viennese Ball for a BBC television programme and they became firm friends. Cliff heard the tragic news when he landed in Copenhagen during a European tour. Cliff's Bentley was to be used to chauffeur Jill to her wedding to Alan Farthing.

But Cliff and their mutual friend Gloria Hunniford paid a fitting tribute, by working to promote Dando's favoured cause, the British Heart Foundation.

Cliff performs in Birmingham as part of the millennium celebrations in 1999. A special lazer show appeared to spin Cliff on the Hope Beacon

The year 2002 proved to be a special vintage – the launch of his wine Vida Nova sold out, as did tickets for the Wanted tour. He built a new home in Barbados and rocked London at Her Majesty The Queen's, Golden Jubilee party.

Appearing alongside Brian May, Eric Clapton, Elton John, Rod Stewart and Paul McCartney, Cliff sang to over one million people thronging the Mall and the Palace grounds.

In conversation later, Cliff was reported to have asked the Queen, "Ma'am, can we do this again?" She replied, "We'll have to ask the gardener."

Cliff performs with Brian May of Queen at the Golden Jubilee Party at Buckingham Palace, 3 June 2002

More than 50,000 empty champagne bottles were collected after the concert, which was broadcast to 60 countries.

Brian May paid tribute to Cliff when he described him as the most consistent hit-maker in the history of the British charts: "He's never repeated himself. He's still that smouldering firework we want to see ignite."

Cliff had been at the pinnacle of showbusiness for a staggering 46 years of Her Majesty's reign.

Cliff with Rod Stewart,
Ozzy Osbourne and
Paul McCartney at the
Golden Jubilee party
at the palace

The Queen smiles into the crowd as she joins Cliff and others onstage at her Golden Jubilee concert at Buckingham Palace, watched by 12,500 guests

Cliff's love affair with Portugal had begun as early as 1961 when he visited his manager Peter Gormley who had invested in property in what was then the little known town of Albufeira. Over the years he found himself gravitating more and more to the Algarve to relax.

Then in the early 90s he saw and fell in love with the Quinta do Moinho, a rambling farmhouse set in 30 acres, believed to be up to 350 years old, and began the process of renovating and rebuilding, including a guest house for friends.

Portugal became the place Cliff retreated to, both to recuperate and prepare for a schedule that remained as hectic as at any time during his career touring, televising and recording.

As was the case everywhere Cliff went, charity work remained a high priority, even on holiday, and local causes on the Algarve dear to him, such as children and disability, were soon benefitting from his commitment.

But perhaps the secret of Cliff's success is that he never stands still; his mind and his ambition are always looking for new challenges and he found a new mountain to climb in the Algarve. He wanted the moribund 30 acres of farmland to be "tidy and productive". It had languished, and his first experiment was to plant fig trees – five acres of them. But within the year he had exchanged syrup of figs for bottles of wine.

The year 2004 saw Cliff return to the Abbey Road studios to film videos – and he embarked on a sell-out tour of the Summer Nights concerts staged at Britain's stately homes, culminating in the Castles In The Air video, which sold 100,000 copies.

It also saw the release of the long-awaited Nashville album, Something's Going On, which consisted of entirely new numbers.

It was an adventure, a departure and a risk. For the first time, Cliff was working with American writers – 21 in all – and producers; strangers who sat down and wrote with Cliff for two whole weeks. He wanted a challenge, he wanted to be tested and he wanted to climb out of his comfort zone and be surprised.

Cliff films at Abbey Road studios, February 2004

None knew who he was, until Devil Woman was played to them and there was instant recognition and rapport.

Cliff remarked at the time, "Whatever happens to this album, I will always consider it one of my best. If it fails to impress, it will be no one's fault but my own." It didn't.

The 76th studio album released by Cliff reached No 7 in the charts and produced three Top 20 hits. Cliff regarded it as the most exciting album he had recorded in a long time.

In 2005, there were more concerts, another tour, the 60th VE Day celebrations in Trafalgar Square and Cliff's 65th birthday. It was 50 years since a 15-year-old boy had first heard Elvis, and been horrified when asked to sing in a school production.

Fifty years after Cliff had played truant to queue for tickets to hear Bill Haley and the Comets at the Regal in Edmonton, London, his father had bought him a guitar for his 16th birthday and the journey had begun.

Half a century later and with more than 50 major tours to his credit, comprising thousands of nights in concert performing to millions, would anyone have begrudged him time to enjoy his homes in Barbados and Portugal, and retirement on the tennis court?

May 2005: Cliff performs at the 60th VE Day celebrations in Trafalgar Square

But it isn't in the man's DNA. He sang in front of the Pope and a million more in Germany in August, enjoyed a quiet birthday celebration in Portugal and began planning a 2006 schedule that would include a Dionne Warwick anniversary show in Los Angeles, an album of duets and rehearsals for yet another tour.

Two's Company saw Cliff record duets with Elton John, Barry Gibb, Brian May, and reunited him with Lulu, Olivia Newton John and Anne Murray. And the wheel was about to turn full circle.

In a book titled Wines Of The World, the authors had described Algarve wine production as 'bottled headaches for tourists'. Within six years of pulling up the fig trees, Cliff's Vida Nova wine was re-writing the encyclopaedias of viniculture.

In 1998 he planted 16 acres with vines cut from the vineyards of the Rhone Valley in France. A year later he watched as 17 tons of grapes were plucked from the vines, still too young to be wine-producing, but in 2000, the Quinta produced 300 bottles.

Cliff at his vineyard near Albufeira, Portugal, August 2006

Cliff's winemaker David Baverstock declared the vineyard's yield would be ready for market with the next harvest.

And it was. Baverstock's verdict was, "it shouldn't be this good." By 2005, less than seven years after planting and four years into production, Vida Nova won a bronze medal at the London Wine Fair and followed it with a silver international award a year later.

Neighbours joined his venture and a thriving co-operative now has the capacity to produce 150 barrels of wine at what is now called Adega do Cantor – the Winery of the Singer.

Cliff unveils his
Square of Fame handprint at
Wembley Arena pavilion,
London, November 2006

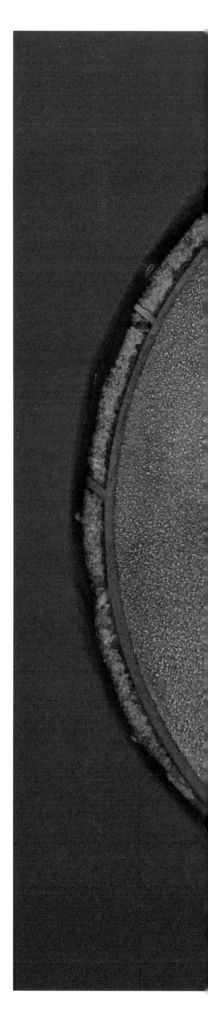

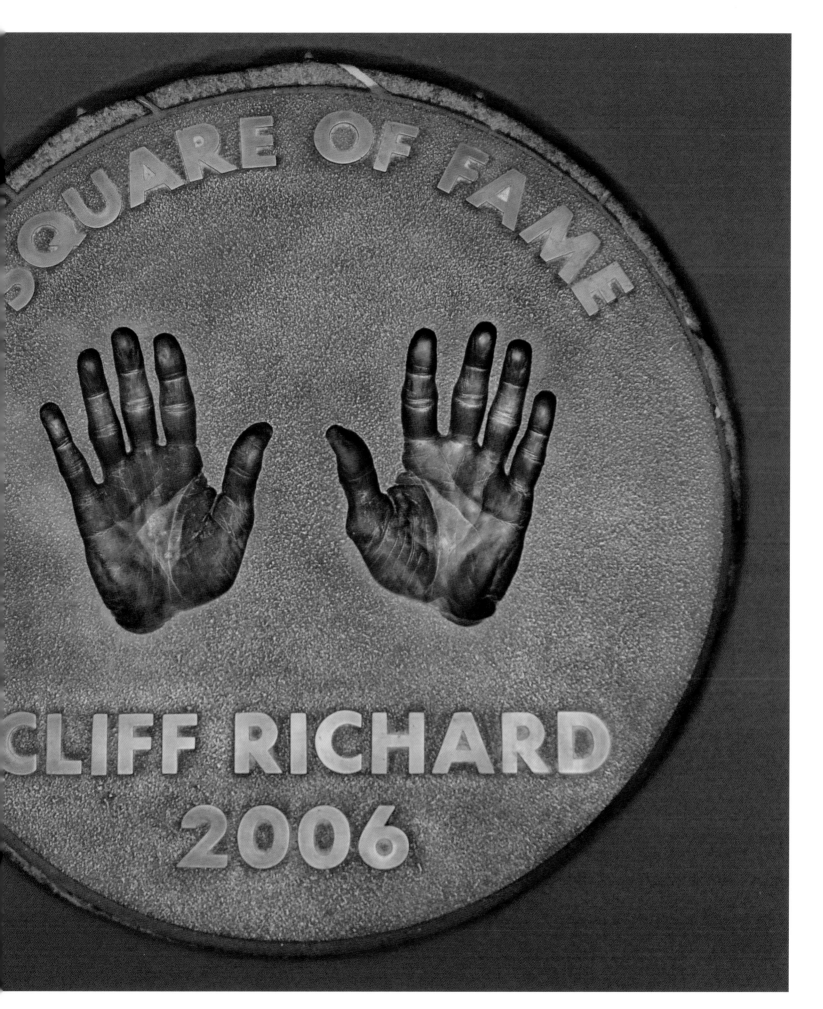

In 2008, the boxed set of And They Said It Wouldn't Last marked Cliff's 50th year of recording. The single Thank You For A Lifetime seemed to suggest Cliff was finally thinking about settling down, pulling the curtains of an unrivalled life in music to a close.

He had been honoured by the Variety Club, the Portuguese government had conferred its own knighthood upon him, the Algarve town of Albufeira named a street after him, he had prepared his official autobiography, and plaques marking his contribution to music and film had been unveiled at the Wembley Square of Fame and Elstree Film Studios.

But then Brian May's "smouldering firework" exploded into action again. Cliff's website announced the news that grabbed the nation's headlines: two decades after their last performance together, Cliff and The Shads were reuniting for an album and a tour.

Cliff in concert at Kirstenbosch Gardens in Cape town, March 2007

They performed a taster at the Royal Variety Show to rapturous applause, recorded the Reunited album – their first studio collaboration for 40 years – and prepared for the road in 2009.

The three-leg, round the world tour took in the UK, Europe, Australia, New Zealand and South Africa, performing live before 617,000 fans. In Britain alone the tour took over £20m. What started in Killarney, Ireland, ended in Johannesburg in March 2010. It had taken in 38 cities and 56 concerts. And the DVD of the tour sold nearly a quarter of a million copies in the UK alone.

What next? Knowing Cliff that's another journey, another book. Watch this space...

Cliff with 'The Shadows' onstage at the London O2 Arena on September 28, 2009

Pages 36-37

Pages 38-39

Pages 40-41

Pages 42-43

Pages 44-45

Pages 46-47

Pages 48-49

Pages 50-51

Pages 52-53

Pages 54-55

Pages 56-57

Pages 58-59

Pages60-61

Pages 62-63

Pages 64-65

Pages 66 -67

Pages 68-69

Pages 70-71

Pages 72-73

Pages 74-75

Pages 76-77

Pages 78-79

Pages 80-81

Pages 82-83

Pages 84-85

Pages 86-87

Pages 88-89

Pages 90-91

Pages 92-93

Pages 94-95

Pages 96-97

Pages 98-99

Pages 100-101

Pages102-103

Pages 104-105

Pages106-107

Pages 108-109

1970's Pages 110-111

Pages112-113

Pages 114-115

Pages 116-117

Pages118-119

Pages 120-121

Pages 122-123

Pages 124-125

Pages 156-157

Pages158-159

Pages 160-161

Pages 162-163

Pages 164-165

2000's Pages 166-167

Pages 168-169

Pages 170-171

Pages172-173

Pages 174-175

Pages 176-177

Pages 178-179

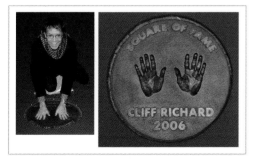

Pages 180-181

Pages 182-183

Pages 184-185